INSANELY PROFITABLE

0-DTE Index Options Trading Strategies

+ 3 bonus readings

XIAO GUDONG

TO

Susan, Angela, and Katerine

TABLE OF CONTENTS

OTHER BOOKS BY XIAO GUDONG

- THE Rational Covered Call Trading Strategy
- THE LONGs And SHORTs of Trading Options
- Learn Crypto From the Wisdom of the Internet
- Insanely Profitable Trading Opportunities
- Stock & Index Options Trading Journal
- 0-DTE Index Options Trading Journal

Thank you for reading the 0-DTE Index Options Trading Strategy. Please leave an honest review of this book.

CHAPTER ONE

ZERO-DAYS-TO-EXPIRATION INDEX OPTIONS

I hope you have already gained some basic knowledge of 0-DTE before starting to read this booklet. If not, I recommend reading my other 0-DTE booklet, Insanely Profitable Trading Opportunities, before continuing. It is even better to do a subject search and read more about the basics of 0-DTE.

Having stated the about, I would like to start the booklet by delving into some of the options trading strategies, especially those most popular among 0-DTE traders. On the Think Or Swim trading platform cell phone version, there are about 15 options and strategies for traders. However, due to the very short time frame for trading, only a few strategies are suitable for 0-

DTE. They are singles, vertical spread, butterfly, iron condor, straddle, and strangle. Some of the above involve complicated pairing; others require longer holding time. Needless to say, traders can choose to go long or short with the strategies, but not every strategy is suitable for both.

For example, if part of our goal is to have a defined risk profile, then neither naked short call nor naked short put is the right choice.

I'd like to know exactly what my risks are and my potential reward for every trade.
I usually do not trade naked singles in or by themselves simply because the daily range of the index is mostly in line with recent trading days in a trend; so-called "unlimited profit potential" is unlikely to happen, especially if we enter the trade after the range of the day is likely already set.

However, I would use naked long when I believe I need some hedge to limit my potential loss further in my primary position. is under pressure due to unfavorable developments. I will cover this strategy in the later chapters.

My primary strategy, which I rely on to double my trading account yearly, is some very basic vertical spreads, plus complimentary naked long singles occasionally.

Before we discuss my recommended strategy in detail, let's examine two other very popular strategies among options gurus.

First, the butterfly.

CHAPTER TWO

THE UGLY SIDE OF A BUTTERFLY

A butterfly position combines a bull and a bear spread. The two vertical spreads share one common strike in the middle with the other two legs on either side. The middle strike needs to have either two long or two short contracts; it can not be one of each. If the middle strike is long, the two flanks are short, and vice versa.

For example: 1 long 559, 2 short 560, 1 long 561.

This essentially consists of a long 559/560 vertical spread and a short 560/561 vertical spread combined. The distance between the long strike (560) and the short strike (559, 561) is $1.

Suppose we paid $0.20 to buy this butterfly and have a potential profit of $0.80. This is a 4:1 profit and loss ratio, quite lucrative, isn't it?

As your brokers would say, the maximum loss for this trade is the $0.20 we paid or $0.20 debit. We lose if the price of this index falls outside of the two shorts (559 and 561). Theoretically, we would have some profit if the price stays between 559 and 561.

Notice that I said theoretically. Yes, the profit potential only exists on paper. Unless the price at the close of the trading session is exactly 560, we will suffer a loss, which is guaranteed!

I will explain this peculiar phenomenon later. Right now, we need to know that there are only two ways to harness a profit during trading hours. One is to pre-set a sell-to-close order and hope it gets filled. The other is always staring at your monitor and placing an exit order when your instinct tells you to. I don't know about you, but neither is desirable to me.

To elaborate further, I turned to the Chatbot and conducted a series of Q&As to articulate the butterfly's peculiar characteristics.

The following is a digest of the part concerning butterfly strategy.

Q: in the long butterfly option strategy, will the breakeven points merge closer and closer before expiration? (I asked this question because I have noticed using real-time P/L simulation that the profit zone of a butterfly trade becomes progressively narrower as the day passes.)

A: No, the breakeven points in a long butterfly option strategy will not merge closer and closer toward expiration.

Here's why:
- *Breakeven Calculation: The breakeven points for a long butterfly are calculated based on the strike prices and the net*

premium paid for the strategy. The breakeven points are:

- *Lower breakeven: Lower strike price + net premium paid*
- *Upper breakeven: Higher strike price - net premium paid*
- *Time Decay: As expiration approaches, time decay erodes the value of the options. This benefits the long butterfly strategy as it reduces the value of the short options in the middle, but it does not change the breakeven points.*

What happens as expiration approaches:

- *Profit Zone Narrows: As expiration nears, the profit zone between the two breakeven points narrows due to time decay.*

Maximum Loss Unchanged: The maximum loss remains the same throughout the life of the trade and is limited to the net premium paid.

Although I was unsatisfied with the answer, it addressed my question directly. The distance between the profit zone does not change. What changed is the probability of profiting from the trade.

I wanted the AI bot to further explain the distinction of the distance between break-even points, which are constant, and the profit zone, which changes. Thus, this follow-up question.

Q: But why the profit zone narrows while the distance between two breakeven points remain unchanged?

A: You've raised a great point! There seems to be a misunderstanding. While the break-even points themselves remain unchanged in a long butterfly spread as expiration approaches, the probability of the underlying asset's price landing within the profit zone decreases. This is due to a few factors:

1. *Time Decay: As expiration nears, the time value of the options erodes. This decay affects the short options in the middle of the spread more significantly than the long options in the wings. As a result, the potential profit from the short*

options decrease, effectively narrowing the profitable range even though the break-even points remain static.

2. *Volatility:* Changes in implied volatility can also impact the profit zone. If volatility decreases, the value of all options in the spread will decline, but the short options will be affected more than the long ones, again leading to a narrower profit zone.

3. *Price Movement of the Underlying Asset:* If the underlying asset's price moves significantly away from the middle strike price, the probability of it returning to the profit zone by expiration diminishes. This effectively narrows the "likely" profit zone, even though the theoretical break-even points remain the same.

Key Takeaway: While the break-even points themselves don't change, the likelihood of profiting from the trade decreases as expiration approaches due to time decay, potential changes in volatility, and the underlying asset's *price movement. This is why the profit zone is often visualized as narrowing over time, even though the break-even points remain fixed.*

The above essentially explains that the profit zone is exactly the distance between the two break-even points at the time the trade order is placed or the time the order is filled. After that, the profit zone starts shrinking. The profit zone will be precisely zero at expiration because zero time values are left on these two long options contracts.

I then went one step further in the conversation asking the question again by actually describing the shrinking phenomenon.

Q: So by looking at the P/L graph the "distance between the breakeven points completely closes up at expiration, which means the probability of profit is zero at that point in time, does it mean if one does not exit the trade before market close then he will have a loss?

A: Yes, you are absolutely correct in your understanding of the P/L graph for a long butterfly spread.

Here's a breakdown of what happens at expiration:

1. *Break-even Points Converge: On the P/L graph, you'll notice that the break-even points seem to merge as expiration approaches. This is a visual representation of the narrowing probability of profit. While the theoretical break-even prices themselves don't change, the likelihood of the underlying asset's price landing precisely between them becomes increasingly small.*
2. *Zero Probability of Profit at Expiration: At expiration, the profit zone effectively disappears. The underlying asset's price will either be:*
   - *Below the lower break-even: Resulting in a loss equal to the initial debit paid for the spread.*
   - *Above the upper break-even: Also resulting in a loss equal to the initial debit.*

- ○
  - ○ *Exactly at the middle strike price: Resulting in the maximum profit, which is the difference between the middle strike and the lower/upper strikes minus the initial debit.*

3. **Guaranteed Loss if Not Exited Beforehand:** *If a trader holds a long butterfly spread until expiration and the underlying asset's price is not exactly at the middle strike, they will incur a loss. This is why it's crucial to exit the trade before expiration if the price movement is unfavorable or if the potential profit has significantly diminished.*

Important Note: The P/L graph is a theoretical representation. In reality, market makers may adjust their quotes near expiration, leading to slightly different outcomes. However, the general principle of decreasing probability of profit and the need to exit before expiration remains valid.

So there you have it.

We might be looking at a more than 10x P/L picture. But it is almost impossible for it to actually happen. The possibility of the index price closing exactly on the options strike at the center is very, very slim

.

In the options world, if we are $0.01 out-of-the-money, we are out-of-the-money.

If one of the vertical spreads closes in the money, the other vertical spread is out of the money. At expiration, it is a wash. In the meantime, we lost the money we had paid for the trade.

It is conceivable that the index price stays at or near the center strike during the trading session. However, the actual profit will not be as high as the "potential" because there will still be some extrinsic value on the contracts before markets close. Also, bear in mind that the size of the profit is progressively smaller closer to the expiration.

The last sentence of the above paragraph is a crucial factor in choosing the strikes in the butterfly trade. Because the potential of a win is greater if the strikes are closer to at-the-money, but the profit percentage will be smaller, likely smaller than 2x.

Conversely, if our goal is to make more than 2x or even near 10x, then the strikes will be way out of the money, significantly lowering the probability of a win.

Conclusion: The butterfly looks pretty on paper.

CHAPTER THREE

OTHER COMPLEX SPREADS

Other popular options trading strategies among gurus include the condor and the Iron condor.

The construct of a condor is similar to a butterfly but with the middle two contracts one or several strikes apart. It has four legs on the P/L graph.

The iron condor also has four legs but uses a call spread and a put spread.

These four-legged spreads all have a defined risk and a defined profit zone, meaning both the risk and potential profit are capped to a certain amount.

These spreads share the same characteristics as the butterfly, where the profit zone diminishes as the trading day progresses. The difference is the profit zone of these four-legged spread does not disappear completely. There will be some profit at expiration as long as the price falls in between the two middle strikes.

However, it is extremely unlikely to achieve the maximum profit as shown on the P/L graph because that will require the price to land exactly at one of the two middle strikes.

I do not use these strategies for 0-DTE because the more "legs" in the contract the more difficult to get filled. The extrinsic value of the options is constantly shrinking, which means our profit potential gets smaller and smaller while we wait for the order to be filled.

The disadvantage of trading multi-legged spread is further magnified by the fact that the "effective" trading range is significantly restricted in the 0-DTE market. There are just not that many "attractive" ranges to trade. Keep in mind that an iron condor requires a span of four strikes to construct. Most indexes that offer 0-DTE options simply do not have swings of more than four points day in and day out.

My vertical spread strategy not only possesses the same capped profit and loss quality and takes much less time to get filled, it is also much versatile in terms of further limiting risks during the course of the day.

CHAPTER FOUR

DEBIT TRADES VS CREDIT TRADE

Debit trades are contracts that we spend money to buy. Our trading account is temporarily debited for the contracts that we acquire. We make money if the price is higher when the contracts are sold or expire. We lose money if the price is lower.

Credit trades are contracts we sell for a certain amount of money. Our trading account is temporarily credited with the amount the contracts are sold for. If the contracts become more expensive when we decide to buy them back or at expiration, we lose the difference.

We can buy a call contract or a put contract. If we pay money to acquire the position, we are long.

We can sell a call contract or a put contract. We don't have to actually own the contacts in our account as long as we buy them back before they expire or we cash-settle the difference with our brokerage after expiration. If we receive money by selling the contracts to establish a position, we are short.

For a single long contract, our maximum loss would be the money we pay. So, the risk is defined, or we can say it is known. Our maximum profit is infinite.

Our maximum profit is the money we receive for a single short contract, and our maximum loss is infinite.

The same concepts apply to any multi-legged position. We are long if we receive a debit when the position is established, and we are short if we receive a credit.

However, depending on how the contract is constructed, the short multi-legged position can also have a defined risk.Almost all options training classes advise against using strategies with an infinite risk profile, and my 0-DTE trading strategy is no exception.

I do not trade naked short options, period.

All my primary positions are paired as vertical spreads. I occasionally use naked long call or long put to complement my primary positions to further limit exposures.

So basically I only trade vertical call or put spreads, and naked long call or put.

CHAPTER FIVE

RISK/REWARD PROFILE OF VERTICAL SPREADS

We will use the mini S&P-500 index, symbol XSP, throughout the booklet.

A vertical call spread consists of a long call and a short call of different strikes.

For example, pairing a long 560 call and a short 561 call is a vertical spread. It is a long position because a 560 call would be more expensive than a 561 call, and we need to pay the difference.

If the spread pairs a short 560 and a long 561, it is a short position. We will receive a credit for the trade.

Regardless of whether it is short or long, it has a defined risk and a capped profit potential.

For example, if we bought a 560/561 call spread and paid $0.49, we would have a ready-known risk of $0.49 and a capped maximum profit of $0.51. Basically, it is a 50:50 profit or loss. Of course, the profit or loss could be smaller, depending on where the price of XSP is at expiration. But it will never be bigger than the defined numbers.

The further the spread goes out of the money, the cheaper the long spread will be. For example, a long 564/565 call will be cheaper than 560/561.

The opposite is true: the more the spread goes in the money, the greater the cost of a long spread will be. The long 555/556 call is obviously more expensive than the long 560/561 call.

For a long vertical call position, the lower the cost (more out-of-the-money), the higher the reward. On the flip side, the more in-the-money, the higher the risk (cost of trade) and the lower the reward.

The above statements are simple math and easy to calculate. If we subtract the premium we pay from the size of the spread, we'll get the possible reward.

But when we stop to think about it. Would it be true if we say for a vertical spread that has a defined risk, the higher the cost, the easier for it to be profitable?

It must be, right? Otherwise, why would it have a higher cost and a smaller reward?

If the answers to the above questions are false, then why would anybody want to pay more for a lower reward?

Following the above "logic," the risk/reward ratio seems to imply future price movement for whatever reason. The higher the cost of a long call, the likelier it is to produce a profit. The higher premium we pay, the lower the possible reward.

Now, why is that? The reason must be in the "likelihood" of making a profit. In other words, traders are willing to pay higher premiums to gain lower profits because the probability of profit is higher. And in order to make high-cost/low-reward trades, traders need to look in the direction of the price trend.

The logic goes like this: The more the spread is out-of-the-money, the cheaper the price and the higher the reward, but the lower the probability of profit. The deeper the spread is in-the-money, the more costly the price is and the lower the reward, but the higher the probability of profit.

And in order to profit from a deep in-the-money long call spread, the price needs to rise further to make the spread even deeper in the money.

To confirm this analysis, I again asked the AI chatbot questions concerning my logics.

Q: Are the following statements true? The further the spread goes out-of-the-money, the cost of a long call spread will be cheaper. For example, long 564/565 call spread will be cheaper than 560/561.

The opposite is true that the more the spread goes in-the-money, the greater the cost of a long spread will be. The long 555/556 call is obviously more expensive than the long 560/561.

For a long vertical call, the lower the cost (more out-of-the-money), the higher the potential profit.

On the flip side, the more in-the-money, the higher the cost of trade and the less the potential profit.

A: Yes, all of your statements are generally true for long vertical call spreads. Let's break down each one with some explanations:

1. Out-of-the-Money (OTM) Spreads Are Cheaper:

- *OTM calls have less intrinsic value (the difference between the strike price and the underlying asset's price) and more time value.*

- *Since time value decays, OTM calls are cheaper than in-the-money (ITM) calls.*
- *A long vertical spread involves buying a lower strike call and selling a higher strike call. When both are OTM, the net debit (cost) of the spread is lower due to the cheaper premiums.*

Example:

- *A 564/565 call spread (both strikes OTM) would generally be cheaper than a 560/561 spread (both strikes closer to the money or ITM).*

2. In-the-Money (ITM) Spreads Are More Expensive:

- *ITM calls have more intrinsic value and less time value.*
- *They are more expensive than OTM calls due to their higher intrinsic value.*
- *A long vertical spread with ITM calls will have a higher net debit (cost) because the bought call is more expensive.*

Example:

- *A 555/556 call spread (both strikes ITM) would typically be more expensive than a 560/561 spread (both strikes closer to the money or OTM).*

3. OTM Spreads Have Higher Potential Profit:

- *OTM spreads have more room for the underlying asset's price to rise and reach the higher strike.*
- *The maximum profit for a long vertical spread is the difference between the strikes minus the net debit.*
- *With a lower net debit (OTM spread), the maximum profit potential is higher.*

4. ITM Spreads Have Lower Potential Profit:

- *ITM spreads have less room for the underlying asset's price to rise before reaching the higher strike.*
- *The maximum profit is still the difference between strikes minus the*

- *debit, but with a higher debit (ITM spread), the potential profit is lower.*

Important Considerations:

- *Probability of Profit: While OTM spreads have higher potential profit, they also have a lower probability of expiring ITM.*
- *Risk-Reward Tradeoff: ITM spreads have lower potential profit but a higher probability of expiring ITM.*

Volatility: Implied volatility affects option prices, so the cost of spreads can vary based on market conditions.

The wonderful thing about having "conversations" with chatbots is that they tend to overdeliver their answers. It is no difference this time. Notice where it says "Probability of Profit." It has literally answered my follow-up question.

Q: You are ahead of my thoughts. I was going to ask you about the probability of profit. Why would anybody want to pay more to get a lower reward? You stated in your answer to my first question that it has a higher probability of profit. Please explain.

A: Not directly, but the cost of a long option position can provide clues about market sentiment and potential price direction. Here's how:

 1. Implied Volatility:
- *The cost of an option (its premium) is heavily influenced by implied volatility (IV), which is the market's expectation of future price fluctuations.*
- *Higher IV means higher premiums, and vice versa.*
- *If the cost of a long position is high, it suggests that IV is elevated, indicating that the market expects significant price movement, but not necessarily in a specific direction (it could be up or down).*
  2. Skew:
- *Skew refers to the difference in implied volatility between OTM calls and OTM puts.*
- *A positive skew means OTM calls are more expensive than OTM puts, suggesting the market expects a*

- *higher probability of upward movement.*
- *A negative skew means OTM puts are more expensive, indicating a higher probability of downward movement.*

3. *Open Interest and Volume:*

- *Open interest (OI) is the number of outstanding option contracts, and volume is the number of contracts traded in a given period.*
- *High OI and volume in a particular strike price or series can indicate market interest and potential price targets.*
- *For example, high OI and volume in OTM calls might suggest that traders are positioning for a potential upward move.*

4. *Put/Call Ratio:*

- *The put/call ratio compares the trading volume of put options to call options.*
- *A high put/call ratio suggests a bearish sentiment, while a low ratio suggests a bullish sentiment.*
- *This can provide insights into market expectations, but it's not a foolproof indicator of future price direction.*

Important Considerations:

- *Multiple Factors: The cost of a long position is just one piece of the puzzle. It's essential to consider other factors like technical analysis, fundamental analysis, and market news to get a comprehensive picture of potential price movement.*
- *Market Manipulation: Large traders or institutions can influence option prices, so it's important to be aware of potential manipulation and not rely solely on option prices to predict price direction.*

In conclusion, while the cost of a long option position doesn't directly indicate the direction of the underlying asset's price movement, it can provide valuable insights into market sentiment and potential price targets. By combining this information with other analysis tools, traders can make

AI chatbots tend to be very conservative in providing answers to questions of controversial subjects. The above Q&A is no exception. Although we did not get a direct yes or no answer, they nevertheless confirmed our conclusion that the cost of the options is a major element for projecting the direction of price movement.

However, this phenomenon only makes sense if the underlying trend continues. That is, the uptrend needs to continue higher so that the premium we paid for the long call contract does not evaporate and that the uptrend also pushes the contract deeper into the money.

CHAPTER SIX

CONTRARIAN THINKING

There is this famous saying about price trends: The trend continues until it reverses, or something to this effect. Numerous technical analysis tools have been invented to define and follow price trends. Numerous technical indicators have also been invented to anticipate where or when a trend ends. Almost all of these tools and indicators are invented based on the belief that price direction is more likely to follow the trend than not.

But we all know price movement is far from parabolic. Stock prices zig zag. Index prices zig zag as well, both in uptrends and in downtrends.

How big are the zig zags? It depends on your perspective. We can find zigzags in monthly charts, weekly charts, daily charts, and even minute charts.

These zigzags cause the premises we laid in the previous chapter about profit probability to lose their validity. In a counter-trend move, the high-cost/high-probability trades turn into losers. And when they lose, they lose big because their high costs suddenly become high liabilities.

For example, suppose we spend $0.65 to buy a one-dollar spread aiming for a $0.35 profit in an uptrend. We are liable to lose as much as the whole $0.65 we paid for the spread if the trend reverses. The depreciation of the extrinsic value adds to our demise.

Does this mean that we should trade countertrends to make money? Not necessarily. There are winners in trend-following trades, too. But personally, I trade almost exclusively countertrends.

CHAPTER SEVEN

THE BASIC TRADES

Before we get into the nitty gritty of my trading strategies, let's examine what the pricing of a contract conveys to us in addition to risk, reward, and probability.

Let's say the current price of XSP is $561 per share. The delta of its at-the-money $561 call or put will be very close to 50%. It effectively means the options at $561 strike will move $0.50 if the XSP price moves $1 in either direction. This also means the price of XSP has a 50-50 chance of moving up or down while everything is equal.

The delta gradually increases for call options at lower strikes (in-the-money) and gradually decreases for options at higher strikes (out-of-the-money). For example, the delta for the 559 strike is higher than 50% and also higher than the 563 strike.

This tells us, in terms of trading, that the price movement of in-the-money options is more aligned with the underlying—or, more accurately, more responsive to the underlying changes.

In a super short-term trading environment like the 0-DTE, the depreciation of extrinsic value should not be our primary objective. Price movement is.

At this point, we have established that the at-the-money contracts have a 50-50 chance of moving up or down, although we don't know how long the move will last or how big it will be. Armed with some basic knowledge of a few trend-following technical indicators, the odds are on our side to win the trades by correctly predicting the trend.

By extension, we can deduce that when the trend direction is a 50-50 chance, paying a premium for a vertical spread that is higher than the possible reward, on average, is a losing proposition.

For a basic at-the-money vertical spread, we can pair one strike below the at-the-money strike and one strike above for a $2 spread. The premium should be around $1. If we believe the trend is up from now, we can sell a put spread or buy a call spread. They work mostly the same, except the individual legs are priced high for call options on most days.

The maximum profit for these trades is around $1 if the underlying moves more than $1 in the direction of our trade at expiration. The maximum loss is also around $1 if the underlying moves against us.

My recommendation for readers who have never experienced 0-DTE is to do a few of these basic vertical spreads. Start with just one contract and, if possible, let the contracts expire without exiting. Your maximum loss/reward is around $100 per contract.

CHAPTER EIGHT

WHAT I DO AND DON'T DO

I do not trade naked shorts because, in theory, the loss is infinite. Although I realize that on most days, the index has a stable trading range, seeing the trade go against me without a known price target negatively affects my confidence.

I do not trade naked longs as my primary position, either. But I often use them as a hedge to reduce my exposure.

For example, if I was long call 562/564 with XSP at 561 and dropping. I may consider a long 562 put to hedge the loss partially. The gain, if any, will offset part of the loss by the long call spread. If XSP turn

Up to above 562, the spread's gain may partially cover the naked long put's loss. Either way, I may be able to stem the loss significantly from this maneuvering.

I trade primarily call vertical spreads, short call vertical spreads, to be exact.

The smallest distance between the long and short ends of XSP is $1.00. If we are long the spread at $0.50, our risk/reward profile is $0.50/$0.50. If we are short the spread at $0.60, our risk/reward profile is $0.40/$0.60. This is elementary.

I set my objective at a risk/reward profile of $0.20/$0.80 or better. This means that I sell short the call spread at a minimum of $0.80 per share or $80 per contact, leaving only $20 per contract of maximum loss. It is effectively a 4x profit-to-loss trade. And I would leave the trade without stop-loss until expiration.

For example, if the trade was long 560 and short 559 for $0.80. The break-even point is 559.80. I will see a loss if the index closes at 559.80 or above. If the index closes above 560, I will see a maximum loss of $20 per contract.

If the index closes below 559, I will gain a maximum profit of $800 per contract.

However, this in-the-money vertical spread is usually two to four strikes below at-the-money. On a low-volatility day, the index might not have the daily range to reach that far out for me to profit.

Short vertical call spreads anticipate the index to go lower. If I expect the index to rise, I will use short vertical put spreads.

However, it has been documented that the index's daily range for an average down day is materially bigger than that for an average up day.

Also, for some unknown reason (to me), the prices of call options are significantly higher than the corresponding put options.

CHAPTER NINE

FINE-TUNING MY STRATEGIES

Generally speaking, the volatility is higher in the first 30 to 45 minutes of a trading day. I sometimes pre-set my order before the market opens for a short vertical call one and two strikes below at-the-money for a price in the $0.91-$0.95 range, depending on how the index is performing in the pre-market.

Eight out of ten times, my order does not get filled in the first few minutes of the opening bell. I will start to gradually lower my asking price to as low as $0.82-$0.85. I will also decrease my contract number so I can keep my total risk within a set limit.

For example, if the $0.92 sell order is for 10 contracts, it will be revised down to 6 or 7 contracts for $0.85. This adjustment is totally discretionary.

I usually do not chase the market down for short orders. If the market drops significantly right off the gate, it may just turn out to be a good opportunity to go long to short a vertical put spread. Again, there are no set rules for the switch of direction. It all depends on how we see the market on any particular day.

Mentally, I treat the 0-DTE trades as informed gambles. Like the zigzags of a trend, nobody knows when and how the market will turn. But we all have some experience in seeing how the market reacts to news items. Some news has a much longer-lasting power to lift the market up for days on end, while others have minimal impact and vanish in a few minutes.

The key is to try to take the most profitable trades and avoid those with unfavorable risk/reward profiles.

I also often use one very effective way to limit further possible loss: to set up an opposite trade to partially offset our loss. The keyword in the sentence is partial.

Previously, I mentioned how I would use naked long calls or long puts to negate possible loss partially.

I can usually identify a "likely" losing trade about two hours before the market closes. At that time, I would order to short a vertical put spread that overlaps one of the strikes of my short call spread.

If I believe my 559/560 short call vertical is likely doomed, I would order one contract of short 560/561 put vertical for $0.45-0.50.

For example, if my five-contract 559/560 short call vertical is at $0.80, and if the index closes at above 561, my total loss to the maximum will be $100. The short put vertical, however, will realize a profit of $0.50, offsetting my loss to only $50 instead of $100.

CHAPTER TEN

THE RANDOM WALK THEORY, MEAN REVERSION, AND AVERAGE RANGE

There is this random walk theory that says the future development of the stock market is totally random and that history has absolutely no bearing on it.

This is a denial of the validity of all technical indicators and economic theories.

It might just be true because, if we think about it, none of the technical indicators is 100% correct, and none of the economic theories developed in the past 100 years can stand the test of time.

However, I subscribe to the mean reversion phenomenon. Mean reversion basically says that price movement will self-correct back to its means, no matter how erratic its recent performance is.

Actually, the zigzags we see on price charts are a result of mean reversion, which provides opportunities to trade countertrends.

In a day-trading environment, counter-trend trades offer a better chance of making a profit and a bigger profit potential. Let's face it: there are only 6 ½ hours in a trading day, and by the time the trend of the day becomes evident, there may not be enough time or space to generate a decent profit.

In addition to the above, we need to be realistic about entering trades with a four-or-more-times-risk-reward ratio, such as a $0.80/$0.20 or even a $0.90/$0.10 vertical spread. These vertical spreads are usually two or even more strikes in the money. The index may not have a swing of this magnitude to reach that far to produce a profit.

One way to determine if the index is likely to reach or exceed our profit point is to check the ATR indicator. ATR stands for Average True Range. It basically shows the average width of the swing in a given period. It is available in most stock analysis software on most trading platforms. The default setting is a 20-day average. I prefer a shorter measuring period of seven days or less.

Always consult the ATR indicator to determine if the index is likely to reach beyond the breakeven point to generate a profit before sending the order.

CHAPTER ELEVEN

SOME MORE DETAIL

I was once taught by a seasoned options trader to exit a winner when it achieves 50% of potential profit. The rationale behind this is that once the profit passes 50% of its potential, the risk becomes greater than the potential reward.

It makes a lot of sense because if the market reverses at any point, we are not only liable to give back all of the profit, but our initial cost of doing the trade is also in danger.

However, the rules of most brokerage houses (or the authority?) stipulate that traders need to have more than $25,000 in net assets in their trading accounts to be eligible to day trade, that is, exit the trades on the same trading day. Without a day trader status, traders are only allowed two day trades in a five-day period.

This is an important factor of why I mostly make high-reward, low-risk trades and only trades with potential loss that I can handle psychologically. This way, I can allow the trades to expire at the end of the day. The funds in my trading account are all discretionary.

One great benefit of letting our contracts expire is that we are free to spend most of our days doing other things.

For the past 3 ½ years of trading 0-DTE, I have had an average win/loss ratio of about 1-3 in the number of trades and a 2.5-1 profit/loss ratio monetarily.

I am a trained technical analyst but I am always skeptical of devising strict trading rules solely by technical analyses. How can one make a solid set of trading rules based on something unreliable as technical indicators?

That is why much of the decision-making in my strategy is discretionary. Readers should start practicing with a minimum number of contracts to familiarize themselves with the behavior of the options contract and the index. We can always up the bet when we are comfortable using our trading strategy.

However, I do have a few guidelines that I try to adhere to.

The first is that I do not use stop-loss orders. I only take trades with a maximum loss that I am comfortable with. I will simply let the trade expire at the end of the day and move on to other possibilities.

The second is that I will at least take one position each trading day unless I am tied by other obligations and unable to be at my monitor, or it is too late in the day, and my orders just can not get filled.

The third one is I will always keep some stock shares in my account. The shares need to be highly correlated to the S&P-500 index to serve as an indicator of the index's direction in the short term. It can also be a hedge against possible losses because the majority of my trades are shorts. Actually, this hedging effect only provides psychological support rather than monetary support. We should treat every position as an independent element instead of part of a whole. However, knowing I have a relatively dependable hedge can significantly boost my confidence in taking short trades.

Why trade the short vertical call spreads instead of the long vertical put spread? For some reasons still unknown to me, the call options are much more richly priced than their counterparts.

CHAPTER TWELVE

CONSISTENCY AND DISCIPLINE

Be conscientious of the fact that we trade only one of the thousands of tickers on the stock market. It is not like having a portfolio of many stocks, each with its own characteristics. So it should be easy for us to stick to just one or two trading strategies.

Here are some of the rules I set up for myself in addition to what was discussed above:

- I do my analysis the night before each day to determine in which direction the index is most likely to move. I then submit an order to trade before retiring for the night. The order is set at a level that is not likely to get filled right at the opening bell. The main purpose of this trade order is to remind me of the result of my analysis the night before so I do not lose sight of the big picture if the market is more erratic than anticipated.

- It is common for me to adjust the trade before the opening based on my assessment of the pre-market movements. I may increase the size of my order, move the trade to other strikes, or adjust my bid/ask prices, but I seldom change direction.

- I will most likely "force" myself to fill an order by adjusting the price and the number of contracts in the first 90 minutes of the day. However, every time I adjust the order, the number of contracts decreases. This is very important; the reason my orders are not filled is because the price of the index is going opposite of my trade. My experience tells me that the orders that are filled later in the day are more likely to be losers.

- I do not keep unfilled orders after three hours into the trading day. If my orders don't get filled at that time, I will cancel them and sit out for the day. The rationale for this is that the extrinsic value of the contracts and the volatility are greatly reduced and that the potential profit is much less attractive.

- The order that I put in the night before is almost always a short call vertical spread, regardless of which direction I think the market will move in the morning. If I believe the market will move higher in the morning, my order will be at-the-money or out-of-the-money. My order will be placed in-the-money if I think the market will move lower in the morning. This is because I place more emphasis on the profit/loss ratio than the probability of profit. Let's face it, we will be very lucky if we guess correctly the market's direction more than 50% of the time. I'd take a 30% probability with a 5x profit ratio over a 70% probability of a 1x profit ratio anytime and every time.

- I will also put in an out-of-the-money short put spread if my analysis points to a strong bull open.

- My trades are always directional. Even if I hold both the short call and the short put positions at the same time, one will be bigger than the other.

The above are a few very simple rules to follow. They work for me, but you can set up your own rules. The key is to be consistent and disciplined.

The Inexorable Rise: What Fuels The Seemingly Infinite Uptrend in the DJIA and S&P Indices?

It is a fascinating phenomenon. We know for a fact that many factors contribute to this incredible trend, such as the economy and the US currency status, as well as the world-dominating military power. However, one often overlooked aspect is the strategic replacement of component stocks within these indexes. This discussion is an attempt to dissect the process and uncover how it biases these indexes toward continual growth. Whether you're a seasoned investor or new to the stock market, understanding this dynamic can provide valuable insights into the nature of these pivotal market indicators.

First, a brief introduction of today's discussion:

The DJIA (Dow Jones Industrial Average) and S&P 500 are not just any stock market indexes; they are the ones that the world closely watches, often serving as indicators of the overall health of the United States economy. A striking feature of both indexes is their method of component selection and periodic replacement, which, I argue, inherently tilts them towards an upward trajectory in the long term. Let us take a closer look at the mechanisms behind this bias, the rationale for stock replacements, and the implications for investors and the broader market.

Both the DJIA and S&P 500 are subject to regular reviews to ensure their components accurately mirror the current market and economic landscape. The

S&P 500, for instance, meticulously selects companies based on market capitalization, liquidity, and industry representation, among other stringent criteria. The DJIA, despite its smaller size of 30 stocks compared to the S&P 500's 500, also strives to represent key sectors of the economy with its selections. When a company in either index significantly underperforms, faces declining business prospects, or is outperformed by another firm that better meets the criteria, an index committee may opt for a replacement.

The replacement process introduces a bias toward growth for several reasons:

1. Performance-Based Selection: Companies facing downturns, bankruptcy, or significant challenges are more likely to be removed. Conversely, those demonstrating robust growth, innovation, and financial health are candidates for inclusion. This ensures that the

indexes gradually phase out weaker performers in favor of stronger ones.

2. Sector Representation: As industries evolve, the indexes adapt by incorporating companies in emerging sectors with high growth potential (e.g., technology and renewable energy). This not only keeps the indexes relevant but also leans them towards sectors with higher return prospects.

3. Market Sentiment and Visibility: Being added to a major index provides a company with increased visibility and often leads to a boost in its stock price due to higher demand from institutional and individual investors. This inclusion effect further contributes to the index's upward momentum.

There are a few definitive long-term implications:

1. This systemic bias towards replacing lagging companies with outperforming ones means that the DJIA and S&P 500 are not merely passive reflections of the market but are dynamically curated portfolios that lean towards growth. Over time, this contributes to the long-term uptrend observed in both indexes. It is important to note, however, that this does not make the indexes immune to market downturns or volatility. Rather, it suggests that their construction methodology helps them recover and reach new highs over the long term.

2. This process of continuous updating makes the indexes more resilient and adaptable to changing economic conditions and technological advancements. It reflects the underlying strength and adaptability of the American economy, as well as the ingenuity and innovation that drive it forward.

3. In conclusion, the frequent replacements of component stocks in the DJIA and S&P 500 introduce a growth bias, contributing to their long-term uptrend. This process ensures that both indexes remain reflective of the evolving economic and market landscape, continuously adapting to include successful companies that drive future growth. For investors, understanding this dynamic provides insight into the nature of these indexes and underscores the importance of innovation and adaptability in driving long-term market performance. Thus, while short-term fluctuations are inevitable, the structural biases of the DJIA and S&P 500 favor a trajectory of growth over the long haul.

But what does it mean to an average investor?

It makes a lot of sense to follow the leaders when considering putting fresh money into the stock market, especially the component stocks of large-cap indexes. The higher they rise, the more weight they carry as a percentage of the indexes. And more investors will be attracted by the rise of the indexes.

In the short term, it could be profitable to invest in smaller companies in a hot sector or industry because of the hype. Most of these smaller competitors will eventually be pushed out or gobbled up by their much bigger competitors. While there is one humongous success like Amazon, there are hundreds of buried bodies along the way.

Always look to the mega-cap leaders on the stock board to determine the underlying market trend. Smart money is more often invested in high-priced names simply because average investors can not afford them, or they are intimidated by their high prices.

When in doubt, put your money in index funds. They have always bounced back, haven't they?

If you do not own APPL, MSFT, GOOG, NVDA, and the like, or you have never made more than double your investment in any stock, chances are very slim that you will ever do it. That is because you just don't have what it takes to strike it big.

In this case, your best alternative is to invest in an index fund, an S&P-500 index fund, to be exact. You are almost guaranteed an 8-10% yearly compounded return without doing any research, without having to trade in and out of the stock market, and most importantly, it is risk-free.

There is no need for any trading strategy, you don't even have to do dollar averaging, just make sure you put your money in as soon as you have them. The only concern is picking the time to cash out. That could be many, many years later.

BONUS READING

#2

Exchange-Traded Funds: A Double-Edged Sword of Financial Innovation

What Is Exchange-traded funds (ETFs)?

Exchange-traded funds (ETFs) represent one of the most significant financial innovations of the past few decades, offering investors the ability to gain diversified exposure to a wide range of asset classes through a single transaction. While ETFs provide financial institutions with lucrative opportunities to earn management fees by packaging and reselling shares, this model also presents inherent risks, including the potential for liquidity crises. This essay examines the operational mechanisms of ETF issuers, explores the risks associated with their business model, and assesses how a liquidity crisis within the ETF market could reverberate through the broader financial system.

Operational Mechanisms of ETF Issuers

ETF issuers operate by creating funds that track the performance of a specific index, sector, commodity, or other asset class. These funds are then divided into shares that are traded on stock exchanges, similar to individual stocks. The creation and redemption process of ETF shares is central to their operation, involving authorized participants (APs) — typically large financial institutions — that have the exclusive right to create or redeem ETF shares directly with the ETF issuer. APs do this by delivering the underlying assets that the ETF is designed to track in exchange for ETF shares (creation) or vice versa (redemption). This mechanism is designed to keep the ETF's market price closely aligned with its net asset value (NAV).

The Lucrative Nature of ETFs for Financial Institutions

For financial institutions, ETFs represent a profitable venture through management fees charged to the fund, calculated as a percentage of the fund's total assets. These fees accrue in exchange for managing the fund's portfolio, marketing and administrative services, and ensuring the ETF accurately tracks its underlying index or assets. ETFs' scalability means that as more investors buy into the fund, the revenue from management fees can grow substantially without a corresponding increase in operational costs.

Potential for Liquidity Crises

Despite the innovative design and operational efficiencies of ETFs, they are not immune to the risks of liquidity crises. Such crises can occur in scenarios where significant sell-offs in the ETF market prompt a large number of redemptions. If

APs are unable or unwilling to facilitate these redemptions — possibly due to difficulties in acquiring the underlying assets or in times of market stress — this could lead to a disconnect between the ETF's price and its NAV. Furthermore, if the underlying assets themselves become illiquid, this exacerbates the problem, potentially leading to a situation where the ETF shares cannot be traded at reasonable prices, causing investor losses and undermining confidence in the ETF ecosystem.

Impact on the Market

A liquidity crisis in the ETF market could have far-reaching implications for the broader financial market. First, it could exacerbate price movements in the underlying assets, leading to increased market volatility. Second, a loss of confidence in ETFs could lead to broader financial contagion, affecting not just individual investors but also institutional participants. In severe cases, this could lead to a reevaluation of the perceived safety and liquidity of ETFs as investment vehicles, prompting regulatory scrutiny and possibly leading to tighter regulations that could stifle innovation and limit the growth of the ETF market.

Conclusion

While ETFs offer financial institutions a profitable platform through management fees and provide investors with a versatile tool for achieving diversified exposure, they are not without risks. The possibility of liquidity crises, though mitigated by the creation and redemption mechanism, remains a significant concern that could have wide-ranging implications for the ETF market and the broader financial ecosystem. As the ETF market continues to grow and evolve, understanding and managing these risks will be paramount for issuers, regulators, and investors alike to ensure the continued resilience and stability of this important financial innovation.

The potential liquidity crises in the Exchange-Traded Fund (ETF) market bear notable similarities to the financial crisis of 2008, often referred to as the "financial tsunami." Both scenarios are rooted in innovative financial instruments and the intricate interplay of market mechanisms, which, under stress, reveal underlying vulnerabilities capable of precipitating widespread financial instability. This comparison sheds light on systemic risks, the role of financial innovation, and the importance of regulatory oversight in maintaining market stability.

BONUS READING

#3

SYSTEMIC RISK OF EXCHANGE TRADED FUNDS

Financial Innovation and Systemic Risk

The innovation of ETFs introduced a new way of investing, offering market participants diversified exposure and the flexibility of trading shares like stocks. However, the mechanisms that make ETFs attractive—such as the creation and redemption process and the involvement of authorized participants (APs)—also introduce systemic risks, particularly in scenarios where market liquidity is compromised.

Similarly, the 2008 crisis was precipitated by financial innovation, notably in the form of mortgage-backed securities (MBS) and collateralized debt obligations (CDOs). These instruments were designed to distribute and manage credit risk but ended up creating a web of interdependencies that made the market vulnerable to liquidity shortfalls.

Liquidity and Market Stress

Potential liquidity crises in the ETF sector could emerge from a disconnect between ETF prices and their net asset values (NAVs), especially if APs face challenges in facilitating redemptions or if the underlying assets become illiquid. This scenario mirrors the early stages of liquidity crises, where market stress leads to a rapid decline in confidence and an inability to liquidate positions at reasonable prices.

The crisis was marked by a severe liquidity shortage, initially triggered by the decline in housing prices and the subsequent loss of confidence in MBS and

CDOs. Financial institutions found themselves holding assets that could not be sold without incurring massive losses, leading to a credit crunch that cascaded through the global financial system.

Role of Financial Institutions

Financial institutions play a critical role in the ETF ecosystem, particularly through APs that manage the creation and redemption of ETF shares. These entities are crucial in maintaining liquidity and ensuring the proper functioning of the ETF market.

Financial institutions were also at the center of the 2008 crisis, both as originators of risky mortgage loans and as investors in the complex securities derived from these loans. Their interconnectedness and the opaque nature of the risks involved amplified the crisis's impact.

Regulatory Oversight and Market Stability

The potential for liquidity crises in the ETF market underscores the importance of regulatory oversight in identifying and mitigating systemic risks. Regulatory bodies must ensure that the mechanisms and practices within the ETF market do not inadvertently contribute to financial instability.

The financial tsunami of 2008 highlighted deficiencies in regulatory oversight, particularly in the shadow banking system and the derivatives market. The crisis led to significant regulatory reforms aimed at improving transparency, reducing risk-taking behaviors, and enhancing the resilience of the financial system.

Conclusion

The examination of potential liquidity crises in the ETF market in comparison with the 2008 financial crisis reveals critical similarities in the role of financial innovation, the dynamics of liquidity under market stress, the central role of financial institutions, and the crucial need for regulatory oversight. While the instruments and contexts differ, the underlying themes highlight the importance of vigilance, transparency, and adaptability in regulatory frameworks to safeguard against future financial tsunamis. Recognizing these parallels can help market participants and regulators alike to better anticipate and mitigate systemic risks in an ever-evolving financial landscape.

This booklet is actually a discussion of my own experience in trading 0-DTE. I did not put too much emphasis on how the chapters are structured.

For the writing of this booklet, I only used Grammarly to check my spelling, punctuation, and grammar. I rejected most of Grammarly's suggestions to improve the persuasiveness of my choice of words and phrases because I didn't want to risk making my logic plain and easy to understand.

I am not trying to make this a best-selling book, and I do not want readers to think of it as another trading strategy book filled with graphs and charts. This booklet lays out the logic of my trading strategies, which have served me well over the past five years. And I just want to share this with retail traders who are serious about making winning trades while having a lot of fun.

It would be deeply appreciated if you would write an honest review after reading this booklet.

Made in the USA
Middletown, DE
29 December 2024

68432909R00046